CONTENTS PAGE

1

WHAT IS MACROBIOTICS

Macrobiotics can be seen to be many things depending on which questions
the inquirer asks, but basically macrobiotics is about achieving and
maintaining a peaceful and co-operative society through each member of
that society regaining his or her biological integrity. This means that
each of us becomes not only disease free, but healthy in a positive sense
of living happily, in harmony with nature and the people around us.

We achieve this state through our way of eating and our way of thinking.
Diet is very important, so in macrobiotics we emphasize whole foods:- the
use of whole organically grown grains and vegetables. We use these to
achieve balance inside us on a physical, mental and spiritual level.
Eventually this sense of balance can become intuitive for us again but we
have lost this faculty and many of us have been eating the wrong foods and
are becoming ill. To regain our intuition we use a conceptual tool- the
polarity between yin and yang. Everything in this universe can be
classified by either yin or yang and this includes our food and
environment; so for instance when it is cold outside we make more warmth
inside our bodies to make balance. We do this by eating more warming and
longer cooked foods.

This booklet deals with macrobiotic desserts. For a more entire picture of
the macrobiotic diet and ways to achieve balance in choosing and cooking
our foods, the following books are useful.

Wendy Esko: Introducing Macrobiotic Cooking: Japan publications.
Wendy Esko: Macrobiotic Cooking for everyone: Japan Publications.
Michele Cowmeadow: Macrobiotic Cooking. Available from contact
Oliver Cowmeadow: Introduction to Macrobiotics: address.
Michio Kushi: The book of Macrobiotics: Japan publications.
Michio Kushi: Natural Healing through Macrobiotics: Japan Publications.

To find out more about macrobiotics you can contact a number of people
listed at the back of this book.

Introduction.

We use desserts in macrobiotic cooking in two ways; as medicine to balance out our condition, particularly if it is overly contracted, tight or yang and simply for enjoyment. It is good if we can combine the two and to accomplish this it is preferable to make light, clean desserts with a clear direction and energy. This for the most part means keeping the ingredients simple and not combining too many ingredients together in any one dish as this creates confusion. The recipes in this booklet range from those suitable for people who are ill and trying to change their condition to those which might be used for celebrations. I have organised it in such a way that people who are not supposed to eat fruit or flour can simply turn to a section of the book which is appropriate to them, or so those who love fruit can easily find a recipe to experiment with.

In order to make health-giving desserts it is best not to use too much oil, either vegetable oil or nut butters, as these tend to clog in the body and prevent the harmonious and clear flow of our energy. Of course there are times when we want this richer quality in dessert; often it is possible to use roast ground sesame seeds or other whole seeds which are more digestible than oil but lend an equally creamy and sumptuous quality to the dessert.

The use of oil in desserts is much more appropriate for winter than for summer because oil helps in our efforts to keep warm, it is also great to use oil or nut butters for parties and other special occasions. Flour also tends to produce a sticky quality and is not easy for the body to digest, so in general it is best to avoid this or use a better quality type flour product such as oatflakes or cous-cous which are more digestible and less refined. Baked flour, in particular, has a heavy, downward and indigestible quality; baked flour does not give the light, upward, yin releasing quality which we seek from desserts and so is generally avoided. I have included a few desserts with baked flour because if you crave that quality it is much better to make your own with good, wholesome ingredients, than that you end up buying a poor quality baked food to satisfy this desire.

Fruit is delicious, particularly in the summer when the body is hot or more yang. Fruit has a cooling effect on the body and also helps remove excess salt, so in the summer fresh fruit, even raw fruit, occasionally is fine for people in good health. Fruit has a very acidic quality and is not easily digestible raw and causes problems for the intestines and kidneys. Because of this we generally try to balance out the acid nature of fruit by combining it with something alkaline. Fire itself changes the quality of fruit, making it a less extreme food and so cooked fruit is much more appropriate for us than raw fruit. In macrobiotic cooking fruit(acid) is balanced by minerals(alkaline) in order to make it more digestible, and so we cook fruit with a pinch of sea salt and often eat fruit in the form of kanten which is made with agar agar, a seaweed gelatin which is rich in minerals.

3

In Macrobiotic cooking we do not include the use of simple sugars such as cane sugar, honey or maple syrup. Cane sugar is a tropical product and so is not a suitable food for us in this climate; also it is highly refined and the minerals which originally grew in the sugar cane have been removed from it and it is no longer a complete food. So in order for our body to be able to digest it, the refined sugar has to take minerals, particularly calcium from our body. Honey is also a very concentrated form of sugar. Both honey and sugar, as simple sugars are absorbed very quickly in the body, mainly in the stomach, and give very quick boosts of energy as the blood becomes saturated with sugar. These quick "highs" of energy are followed by intense "lows" as the sugar is used up and in the process absorbs minerals from the body.

We choose to use comparatively less refined sugars which derive from grains e.g. barley malt and rice syrup. These complex sugars still contain some minerals and are absorbed slowly and harmoniously by the body giving us a much more steady and long term energy. Barley malt and rice syrup are refined from grains which grow in our own, temperate climate. These grains are the seeds of the rice or barley plant and so contain all that dynamic energy which a seed needs in order to grow into a plant. It is this powerful and strengthening energy which we take into our bodies when we eat whole grains or whole grain products, and so with barley malt extract or rice syrup, they are much better for us than sugar or maple syrup. Often in the making of maple syrup chemical pellets are inserted into the trees to increase the flow of sap and so a large percentage of maple syrup is impure.

At times, particularly when beginning macrobiotics, it is tempting to over-use barley malt and rice syrup when we crave a sweet taste rather than learning to cook our vegetables in such a way as to bring out their beautiful, natural, sweet flavour. Craving for sweetness doesn´t have to be satisfied by eating dessert but can be by vegetable quality sweet. A few simple recipes to bring out the sweetness in vegetables are Nishime(waterless) cooking, baking and steaming, as well as in stews. These recipes can be found in "Introduction to Macrobiotic Cooking" by Wendy Esko and "Macrobiotic Cooking" by Michele Cowmeadow. Root and round vegetables- particularly whole carrots, parsnips, onions or pumpkin are extremely sweet if well cooked and are healing, strengthening and soothing as well.

In dessert cookery barley malt and rice syrup can be used to satisfy different conditions. If our bodies condition is overall more contracted, tight and yang then barley malt which has an upward, dispersive and generally more yin energy or nature is the most appropriate sweetener for us to use. If our general condition is looser, more watery and expanded or yin, then rice syrup which has a more settling, balancing effect on the body, is the most appropriate to use. This can make quite a lot of difference to someone´s overall condition, particularly if they are making recovery from a serious illness.

As we change to the macrobiotic diet it takes a while for us to adjust to such different food quality and our bodies often tell us that they want foods from our past way of eating. There are many macrobiotic foods which we can use to satisfy these cravings and it is good that you should be aware of them to help you make the most of your health and this new way of eating which you have chosen.

If you are a healthy person starting macrobiotics who craves sugar and chocolate perhaps you can wean yourself from these by using maple syrup or carob. Carob contains a lot of sucrose naturally but at least it still contains minerals and so during absorbtion does not rob the body of its mineral supply. If you would like to be or need to be more careful of what you eat, dried fruit can be used to satisfy a craving for sugar and chocolate. Raisins are particularly good for this and can be simmered for quite a long time with a pinch of salt for a sweet taste. A very good recipe is whipped raisin kanten which I have included in this booklet.

It is important for you to realize that what you crave when you crave cane sugar is that quick burst of energy we get from it- the trouble is that everything that has a front has a back, and so you can also experience an incredible low or depression some while after eating sugar also. Using macrobiotically recommended sweet quality foods you will become more balanced, have greater endurance of energy and not experience these peaks and trophs physically, emotionally and mentally.

For chocolate cravings mousses made from dandelion coffee with the addition of roast, ground sesame seeds can give that rich, oily sweetness which chocolate has. I have included two or three different recipes using grain coffee.

In macrobiotic cookery we do not use dairy foods because they are made from cow´s milk which is produced by the cow to enable the calf to grow up into another cow. If we wish to be human beings we have to eat food for human beings and not for calves. Milk and milk products contain a lot of saturated fat and help create serious disease.

In cravings for dairy foods, soya products are often substituted, but these are of rather an extreme quality(very yin) and so should be used only very occasionally with awareness that they are pleasurable rather than healthful. Instead, if you are healthy, amasake is a good substitute for dairy; it is rich and consequently mucous-forming but it is also quite a good quality of light, expansive yin energy. If you have to be careful of what you eat rich vegetable sweetness such as onion, chestnut or squash (pumpkin) puree really can satisfy a craving for dairy food. Grain milks can also be used as substitutes, for example oat or rice milk with roasted ground sesame seeds to lend a richer flavour.

If you find yourself craving bread or pastries dry or fresh mochi can be a very appealing substitute, and I have included recipes for this in the booklet. A lot of interesting cakes can be made using cracked and whole grains, for instance bughur wheat, millet, rice and cous cous can all be used to make lovely cakes of varying texture and consistency with or without the need to bake them. Often we prefer not to bake our food because baking lends a very heavy, condensed quality to food. Particularly in desserts we are looking for a lighter or more yin quality and because baking doesn´t satisfy this need, we are often tempted to eat more baked foods rather than seek a lighter and more appropriate quality dessert.

In general desserts are recommended about three times a week although some people may be recommended dessert less frequently or not at all, depending on their condition which they will have created through their past eating.

Although we use and enjoy using fruit in macrobiotic cooking we certainly tend to regard fruit, nuts and desserts generally as a more peripheral part of the diet. In macrobiotic cooking we cut out the extremely contractive foods such as meat and eggs and the extremely expansive foods such as sugar, chemicals and drugs. Our idea is to create a more harmonious and clean blood condition by balancing foods which are by nature more balanced anyway. The principle food for creating and maintaining a balanced blood quality and therefore body condition is whole grain, so at least 50% of our diet is composed of whole grain. Next in importance are vegetables, beans, seaweeds and soups seasoned with miso. Fruit, nuts and seeds are not essentials in the diet but are used when appropriate to give us a more varied and satisfying diet.

Fruit can be used creatively in our diet to relax us and to calm down excess energy which has been produced from a more yang cause, such as when we have been very busy and rushing around a lot, or working hard at a project in a concentrated manner. As fruit tends to diffuse and relax our powers of concentration it is ideal to use at times when we wish for this effect. It is good for us to realize that fruit is not always beneficial; such as at times when we require a lot of clarity and mental agility or at times when we are generally trying to collect our energies together looking ahead to a creative day, such as at breakfast time.

Please enjoy experimenting with these recipes and create new recipes from ideas which I have given; no recipe is appropriate for all people and occasions, but should be adapted to your condition, the weather and what kind of quality will actually suit you. I find so much of the fun in cooking comes from making something I have never made before by slightly changing the ingredients, combination or method of preparation. In the summer more watery, cooling desserts become appropriate; in the winter, a dryer and perhaps more warming dessert, such as rice pudding.

GRAIN DESSERTS

Using grains in desserts containing fruit, nuts and sweetener is a more balanced way of eating dessert. For winter grain puddings are particularly appropriate as they are warming to the body at the same time as creating sweetness. Simple grain desserts can be made for those who are recovering from sickness and do not wish to take fruit in their diet as the very yin or expansive nature of fruit can in some cases stop or retard the healing process of disease. These grain desserts include rice cream, mochi and amasake and I have included other fruit free grain desserts as well.

For making winter desserts it is fine to pressure cook the grain that is used as the basis of the pudding, but in the summer when we are looking for lighter quality foods perhaps boiling would be a better alternative. If a dessert is made too heavy or yang through pressure cooking or baking not only will it not satisfy your need for a sweet relaxing dessert but you will find yourself eating far too much of it.

Perhaps, initially, it will seem as if grain desserts take a lot of preparation in terms of time but so often we will use grain left over from breakfast porridge or the previous days evening meal, that this is not true. In this way a grain based dessert can often be made in 30-40 minutes.

RICE DESSERTS

RICE RAISIN ROYALE

1 cup of short grain rice
1 cup sweet brown rice
5 cups of water
2 pinches of sea salt
1 cup of raisins
2 tbsp. rice syrup or barley malt (optional)

Wash the rice and place it in a pot with water, sea salt and raisins. Bring to a boil and simmer on a low flame until the rice is creamy, between one and one and a half hours. At the end of cooking add sweetener, if rice syrup is cooked for long it tends to lose its sweetness. Place the rice in a serving bowl and serve with roast chopped walnuts or almonds.
      Variations:- This dish is nice served with a light, walnut kuzu sauce or a sauce made with roast and ground sesame seeds and perhaps a little sweetener. In the summer a sauce made with the juice and rind of

one lemon would lighten this dessert and make it more refreshing; the
lemon could also be added to the dessert itself.

JUICY APPLE RICE SQUARES

1 cup of short grain rice
2 1/2 cups of water
2 pinches of sea salt divided
2 cups of dried apple
3 cups of apple juice
2 tablespoons of kuzu
1/2 cup of roasted almonds

Wash and pressure cook the rice with 2 cups of water and a pinch of salt
for one hour. Meanwhile simmer the apples, apple juice and remaining pinch
of salt until soft, about 20-30 minutes. Combine rice and apples and
dilute kuzu in the remaining 1/2 cup of water and add this to the rice and
apples. Simmer for a few minutes . Roast and chop the almonds and sprinkle
these to make a thin cover at the bottom of a square or oblong mould. Pour
in the rice and apple kuzu and allow to set for at least 3 hours. Turn out
the mould and cut it into squares which could be decorated with nuts,
seeds or a thin slice of lemon.
    Variations:- For a firmer setting rice square add a tablespoon of
agar agar. For a spicier taste add a little ginger juice or lemon rind at
the end of cooking. Almost any other dried fruit would be delicious in
this recipe, particularly hunza apricots, raisins or sultanas. In the
summer lightly cooked fresh fruit such as apples or strawberries could be
used with the addition of a little sweetener.

RICE CREAM

1 cup of short grain brown rice
5 cups of water
1 pinch of sea salt

Roast the rice in a dry frying pan and pressure cook it for 1 1/2 hours.
Allow the rice to cool and squeeze it through 3-4 layers of cheesecloth.
Sweeten either with rice syrup or barley malt. After squeezing the rice
through muslin simmer it for about 15 minutes. This rice cream is very
good for sick people, for those in good health it is fine to put the rice
through a mouli to obtain the cream. The bran part can be saved and used
in stews, soups or baking.

AMASAKE

1 cup of brown rice or sweet brown rice
3 cups of water
1 pinch of sea salt
1/4 cup of koji

Wash and soak the rice overnight. Pressure cook the rice with the water
and salt for one hour. Allow the rice to cool until when you put your
fingers in it you can count to five slowly and add the koji. Yellow koji
should be used for making amasake, green koji is for making miso. Mix in
the koji and cover with a damp towel. Let the rice sit in a warm place for
4-6 hours and stir it roughly every 1 1/2 hours. After this time the
amasake should be sweet tasting, if it isn't leave it a little longer.
When the amasake is ready bring it to the boil and simmer for about five
minutes to stop the fermentation.
    Variations:- Any grain can be used to make amasake. If you want to
make amasake drink the rice should be cooked with about 6 cups of water. A
little ginger juice can be nice with amasake drink. For a smoother cream
amasake can be put through a mouli or food mill. Amasake is pretty mucous

forming and is not recommended for people with a lot of dairy excess.

SQUASH AND AMASAKE DESSERT

SQUASH PUREE

1 medium hokkaido pumpkin or other sweet winter squash
1 cup of water
1/4 cup of rice syrup or barley malt
3 tbsp. of kuzu
1/4 tsp. of sea salt

AMASAKE CREAM

4 cups of amasake
1 tbsp. kuzu
1 tbsp. agar agar flakes

Wash, peel and cut the pumpkin into chunks. Put the squash in a pressure cooker with water and salt and pressure cook 15 minutes once it has come to pressure. Put the squash through a mouli or food mill and heat again with kuzu and sweetener until it is thick. Allow the squash puree to cool. If the amasake is thick use it as it is but if it is quite runny heat it with the agar agar for 10 minutes, dilute and add the kuzu, and simmer for about 5 more minutes. To serve layer the amasake cream and pumpkin puree alternately in a dessert glass and garnish with a piece of ginger candy, lemon peel or roasted nuts.

RICE DELIGHT

1 1/2 cups of cooked brown rice
1/2 cup sesame seeds
1 1/2 cups fresh or dried fruit
2 tbsp. rice syrup
1 cup of oat milk
chopped nuts.

If you are using dried fruit, wash and soak this with a pinch of salt for a few hours before preparing the dessert. If you are using large pieces of dried fruit such as whole apricots these can be finely chopped. Combine the fresh or dried fruit with the oat milk in a pan and if using fresh fruit add a pinch of salt. Simmer for a few minutes, add the rice syrup and cooked rice and simmer for a few minutes more. This dessert is particularly nice with soft rice leftover from porridge at breakfast. Place the dessert in a serving dish and garnish with roast nuts, blanched cherries or your favourite garnish. This dessert is particularly attractive if it is made with red or orange fruits or a combination of the two as this makes a lovely colour. My own summer favourite is a blend of strawberries and peach slices. Some of the strawberries can be mashed to give the dessert an overall pink colour.

SWEET CORN AND RICE CREAM DESSERT.

6 ears of fresh corn
1 cup of brown rice
3 tbsp. of rice syrup
2 pinches of sea salt
5 cups of water

Bring the water and salt to a boil. Wash the corn and take it from the cob by slicing vertically down the cob. Simmer the cobs in the water for a couple of minutes and then discard them. Simmer the corn for about 5 minutes, then sieve them out of the water and puree them in a food mill or blender. Wash the rice and simmer it with the cooled corn water for about 1 1/2 hours. Allow the rice to cool and cream it through a mouli, saving the bran parts for soups, stews and baking. Combine the rice and corn cream with the rice syrup in a pan and simmer for a few minutes. Place in individual dessert glasses and garnish.
      Variations:- Raisins or sultanas could be added to this dish. The rind and juice of a lemon will lighten this dish a lot and make it more appropriate to the warm september weather which often comes with the ripened corn.

SWEET RICE DESSERTS

Sweet rice looks very much like ordinary short grain brown rice but contains more protein in the form of gluten. It is this gluten which makes it possible to use sweet rice in interesting and unusual ways. One of these ways, invented by the Japanese, is pounding sweet rice to make mochi, the name given to sweet rice when the individual grains of rice have been pounded so much that they have broken down into a glutinous mass. This mochi can be used to make some interesting and attractive desserts.

SWEET RICE MEDLEY

1 cup of sweet brown rice
1 cup of winter squash
1/4 cup of aduki beans
1/2 cup of dried chestnuts
sea salt

Soak the aduki beans and chestnuts for 3-4 hours after you have washed them. Wash the rice and combine the rice, beans and chestnuts. Wash and slice the pumpkin or squash and add this to the rice. Using the chestnut and aduki soaking water, add 1 1/2 cups of water to each cup of grains, beans or chestnuts and a pinch of salt for each cup as well.Pressure cook for one hour, remove and serve. This makes a delightful and warming winter dessert, it has a lovely natural sweet flavour. This dessert is not really very appropriate for the summer unless it is very cold because long-time cooking together with pressure cooking makes a very heavy dessert, strong in downward energy with a tendency to increase rather than cool the energy in our body.

Variations:- sweet rice, aduki beans and raisins is a delicious combination. For extra sweetness rice syrup or barley malt can be added, also a little ginger juice can add lightness to the dessert. A garnish of a sour or tart nature would also be good, perhaps a little lemon rind or more bitter nuts such as walnuts.

MOCHI

1 cup of sweet brown rice
1 1/4 cups of water
pinch of sea salt.

Pressure cook the rice with sea salt and water when it has been washed. Sweet rice has the same cooking time as ordinary brown rice, so pressure cook it for 45 minutes. When the pressure has come down place the rice in a sturdy bowl and pound it with a fairly heavy round ended piece of wood, such as a suribachi pestle. Continue pounding for about an hour, if the gluten gets very sticky sprinkle on a little cold water and continue pounding. The addition of too much water will make a very runny mochi which is difficult to handle unless left for a few hours to dry out again.

Your mochi is now ready. On its own mochi is not very digestible, so usually another taste and energy of food is combined with it to create some very delicious desserts. Before pounding sweet rice could be cooked with chestnuts or adukis or raisins. Sometimes sweet rice is delicious cooked with an umeboshi plum instead of sea salt. There are a few different dishes which can be made after pounding, some of which I shall explain below.

MOCHI BALLS

Mochi is rather pretty served as little balls. To make it into balls the mochi needs to have been left out to harden for a few hours. Wet your hands so that the mochi does not stick to them and roll the appropriate amount of mochi between your fingers until it has made a nicely shaped sphere. Mochi balls can be rolled around balls of chestnut puree, aduki bean puree, raisin puree, pumpkin puree or apple butter.

or it can be rolled in roast ground sesame seeds, roast, chopped sunflower seeds, pumpkin seeds,almonds or walnuts. Mochi can be rolled in Kinako(roast soya bean flour) and decorated with a hazelnut, a piece of ginger candy or finely grated lemon peel. Mochi is made particularly digestible in combination with a bitter, sour or salty flavour. Mochi balls are rather delicious when they are wrapped around onion butter seasoned with a little miso and umeboshi plum. They can be decorated with finely cut strips of nori. Mochi balls can be deep-fried and served with a ginger and shoyu dip sauce which can be made with one part shoyu to four parts water and four parts ginger.

MOCHI SWISS ROLL

Occasionally I have made this dish and children seem to particularly like it. I use rice paper to roll the mochi in, rice paper is not particularly good quality as it contains potato starch as well as rice but on the odd occasion it is really nice to use for a decorative dessert. Lay the rice paper out on a sushi (bamboo) mat and cover to within half an inch of top and bottom with mochi. On top of this layer any choice of sugarless jam or fruit in a kuzu sauce, nuts roasted and chopped could also be added or lemon rind for a sharper flavour. The nicest jams to use are red or orange ones for colour contrast. Using the sushi mat roll the rice paper round into a spiral until you have a swiss roll shape. To cut, wet a sharp knife. If the knife is not wet the rice paper will tear and the mochi will stick to the knife. Each piece of swiss roll could be lightly dusted with Kinako(roasted soya bean flour) to prevent it sticking, and served decoratively on a large plate.

MOCHI SUSHI

Mochi sushi is very similar in principle to the swiss roll except that nori seaweed which has been toasted is used to roll the mochi in, instead of rice paper. Traditional fillings include roast ground sesame seeds made into a paste with miso and water and perhaps a little ginger or umeboshi plum for variation; roast ground walnuts made into a paste with miso or chestnut puree with a little ginger juice or lemon or orange peel to give a more spicy flavour. For directions on how to make sushi follow those for the swiss roll in the recipe above.

BAKED MOCHI

Mochi can be baked in a medium oven until it puffs up. It can then be cut in half and spread with various fillings.

SWEET RICE AND CHESTNUT DESSERT.

1 cup of sweet brown rice
2 1/2 cups of water
1 pinch of sea salt
1/2 cup of currants
1/2 cup of alexia raisins
1/2 cup of almonds
1 cup of dried chestnuts.

Soak the sweet rice in one cup of water overnight. Combine with the rest of the water, the sea salt, raisins and currants and pressure cook for 30 minutes. Allow the pressure to come down naturally and layer the mixture at the bottom of a casserole.

Soak the chestnuts for at least 4 hours and simmer them for one hour with a piece of kombu and soaking water to cover. Remove the kombu and cook the chestnuts for about another hour, seasoning with sea salt after about 30 minutes. At the end of cooking there should still be some cooking water left to use in making the puree. Puree the chestnuts in a suribachi and add the cooking water until the puree is of a desird consistency. Cover the rice with the puree and decorate with either whole or chopped almonds and bake in a medium oven 20-30 minutes.

This is definitely rather a heavy dessert because it combines both pressure cooking and baking, but it can be appropriate at times when we crave baked flour, this type of dessert is a much better quality downward energy to take. This dessert could also be appropriate in the winter, especially to someone doing heavy physical work outside. For a lighter dessert, this recipe could be used without the baking and with ginger or lemon juice and rind added to the chestnut puree.

OATS

Out of whole grains oats make the creamiest desserts but also the most mucous forming, particularly oatflakes, this is because of their higher fat content. I use oat groats quite often to make a grain milk which can be used as the basis of a dessert. Oatflakes are very useful for making a quick dessert and is particularly delicious when made into a mould.

OAT AND ALEXIA RAISIN MOULD

1 cup of medium oatflakes
2 1/2 cups of water
Pinch of sea salt

1/2 cup of alexia raisins
1 1/2 cups of water
pinch of sea salt
1/2 cup of nuts or seeds.

Bring water, oatflakes and sea salt to a boil and simmer on a gentle flame for 20-30 minutes, stirring occasionally to prevent burning. Set aside. Simmer the raisins, water and sea salt until all the water is absorbed. Puree the raisins in a suribachi and stir in the oatflakes. Line a mould with roast, chopped hazelnuts or almonds and pour in half the oatflake mixture, layer in more nuts or seeds and pour in remaining oat mixture. Allow the mould to cool for 2-3 hours, this is rather nice lightly chilled, and turn onto a plate. For a very simple glaze heat a little barley malt and water and pour over the set mould .
                    Variations: Any fruit can be used with the oatflakes. If you are not going to use a grain sweetener, dried fruits are best because they have a more naturally sweet taste. For people who do not wish to eat fruit this oat mould is delicious made with grain coffee, walnuts and rice syrup.

STRAWBERRY OAT CREAM

1 cup of whole oats
4 cups of water
pinch of sea salt
1 large punnet of strawberries
1/2 cup of water
pinch of salt
2-3 tablespoons of rice syrup

 wash the oats carefully and soak them for about four hours in the four cups of cooking water. Add a pinch of salt and pressure cook for 1-1 1/4 hours. Allow the pressure to come down and when the oats have cooled sufficiently put them through a mouli to make oat cream. Add 2 tablespoons of rice syrup or more if this is to your taste.

Wash and slice the strawberries. Bring 1/2 a cup of water to a boil with a pinch of salt and, leaving a few strawberries aside for a garnish, simmer the strawberries for a few minutes. Add the remaining tablespoon of rice syrup and simmer for 2 minutes more. Either puree the strawberries or mix them as they are with the oat cream and decorate with the strawberries and perhaps a few strawberry or rose leaves if you can find them.

CORN

Corn is, of course, seasonal, so we can only use fresh sweet corn for about two months of the year but it makes a delicious dessert. Apart from whole fresh corn we sometimes use cornmeal to make desserts. Although strictly speaking cornmeal or polenta should be included under flour, it is still much more digestible and appealing than a baked flour dessert.

FRESH CORN PUDDING

12 ears of corn
1/4 lb of Amasake
4 tbsp. of raisins
4 tbsp. of roasted almonds
1 1/2 cups of water
2 pinches of salt.

Wash and cut the corn from the cob. Bring 1 1/2 cups of water to a boil with 2 pinches of sea salt and simmer the cut corn for 5-10 minutes. Remove the corn and save the corn water. Puree the corn to a cream in a food mill or liquidizer. Add the raisins to the corn water and simmer until all the water is absorbed. Mix the raisins, amasake and corn cream and serve in individual dessert glasses with roast almonds to garnish.

SWEET CORN CAKE WITH RAISIN TOPPING.

1 cup of cornmeal
3 cups of water
1 pinch of sea salt
2 tbsp. rice syrup.

Dry roast cornmeal in a frying pan, this helps to bring out the sweetness and make it more digestible. Bring water and salt to a boil and add it slowly to the cornmeal to prevent lumping. Cornmeal tends to foam up while it is cooking so a large saucepan will be needed. Simmer the cornmeal on a low flame for about 40 minutes, stir it regularly as it has a tendency to burn. Put the cornmeal in a rinsed mould and leave it for 2-3 hours to set.

1 cup of raisins
3 cups of water
2 tbsp. of kuzu
1 pinch of salt.

Wash and soak the raisins with salt and water for about two hours. The salt brings out the sweetness of the raisins and the soaking lessens the cooking time, this makes it possible to make a topping with very light energy. Simmer the raisins for 15 minutes and add kuzu, simmering for a few minutes more. Turn out the corn cake and spread with the raisin topping. Cut into slices and serve.
   Variations: Any fruit or nut sauce can be used as a topping for this cake. Fresh fruits in season, particularly orange and red ones for colour contrast, can be used. With fresh fruits perhaps a little rice syrup or barley malt will be needed. The corn cake can be made a little richer and served on its own. Chopped, roasted walnuts, stirred into the corncake when it has finished cooking are lovely. More walnuts could be used as a garnish to serve this cake.

MILLET.

Millet is a very useful grain for making all sorts of moulds both savoury and sweet. Once cooked it can also be baked for a heavier or richer cake like quality. for a baked cake millet, chestnuts and rice syrup go very well with a little ginger to add some lightness.

APPLE AND SULTANA MILLET CAKE.

1 cup of millet
3 cups of water
1 cup of sultanas
2 tablespoons barley malt
2 pinches of sea salt

2 red apples
1 cup of water
1 pinch of sea salt
1 tbsp.barley malt
1tbsp of kuzu

Bring 3 cups of water, salt and sultanas to a boil. Meanwhile wash and dry roast the millet until it releases a nutty fragrance, this helps bring out the natural sweetness of the grain. Add the millet to the water and sultanas, turn the flame very low and leave for 40 minutes. All the water should have been absorbed by the millet. Add barley malt and turn the millet into a rinsed mould, leaving it to set for 2-3 hours.

Heat the water and a pinch of salt. Wash, core and cut the apples into thick half-moons. Add the barley malt to the boiling water and cook the apples for about 2 minutes before removing them. Dilute the kuzu with a little cold water and add this to the apple water until it makes a clear sauce. Turn out the millet cake and decorate it with the slices of apple. Pour the barley malt kuzu sauce over this and allow it to set before serving.
    Variations: All kinds of fruit and nuts can be included in this cake. It is a very nice recipe to use if you are making a conventional two-layer birthday cake; just make two circular millet moulds, allow them to set and add a layer of icing in between. Chestnut icing is delicious, this is just a light puree, perhaps with a little ginger juice also.

WHEAT

Wheat has such a long cooking time that we rarely use th whole grain to make dessert. Instead we like to use bulghur wheat which is a cracked grain. This is very versatile, it can be used to make cakes and steamed puddings as well as very simple desserts.

BULGHUR AND HAZELNUT PUDDING

1 cup of bulghur wheat
2 1/2 cups of water
1 pinch of salt
2-3 tbsp. of barley malt
1/4 lb hazelnuts

Bring water, salt and barley malt to a boil and pour this over the bulghur wheat which should be placed in a saucepan with a tight fitting lid. Cover the saucepan with the lid and leave the bulghur to sit for 20 minutes. It should cook in its own steam. After 20 minutes try the bulghur and add the hazelnuts which should have been chopped and roasted. If the bulghur seems to need it you can cook it for about 5 minutes and add more barley malt if this seems required. Spoon the bulghur into individual dessert glasses and decorate with a few hazelnuts.
    Variations: There are almost infinite possibilities with this dessert so do experiment. Just remember to keep the ingrdients simple, that is the most important rule. Any nuts or fruits could be used in this pudding, dried raisins or currants are really good; apricots, particularly hunza apricots are delicious (they have to be cooked and de-stoned first). A lemon and walnut bulghur dessert is a delicious idea.

BARLEY.

Whole barley isn´t often used for desserts because of its chewy quality.
The way I always use it is as a cream because then it has a much lighter
energy than rice and a clean, refreshing quality which oats with their
higher fat content do not have.

BARLEY PARFAIT

1 cup of barley
4 cups of water
1 pinch of sea salt
2 tbsp. of rice syrup.

2 cups of apple juice
1 cup of chopped dried fruit
3 cubed pears
1 pinch of salt
1/2 cup of roasted nuts
1 1/2 tbsp. of agar agar

Wash and soak the barley for 4-6 hours. Pressure cook with the water and
salt for 1 hour. When cool puree the barley in a mouli and add rice syrup.
Chop the roasted nuts very finely and mix with the barley. This makes a
delicious winter dessert on its own; for the summer the addition of fruit
makes a better balance.

Simmer the apple juice, dried fruit, agar agar and salt for 20 minutes.
Add the pear cubes and simmer for 2 minutes. Set aside to cool. Spoon
alternate layers of fruit and barley cream into dessert glasses. Choosing
an orange or red fruit adds to the colour contrast between fruit and grain
cream. A really nice variation here is pear and blackberry or cherry.

FRUIT DESSERTS.

Fruit is best used fresh only when it is in season in our own climate, so generally we avoid using imported fruits, especially those which have come from a tropical country. This is because tropical fruit is very watery, yin and has a dispersive effect in our bodies, much more extreme than the effect of locally grown fruit. In the winter we tend to use much more dried fruit; the drying of fruit tends to make its energy slightly more contractive or yang. People often have a tendency to use too much dried fruit, for example, a couple of pieces of whole, dried apricots, pears or peaches are plenty for each person for a dessert.

SPARKLING PEACH CONDE

3 cups of rice cream
3 tablespoons of rice syrup

3 large fresh peaches
3 cups of water
1 pinch of sea salt
6 cherries
1 tbsp. of kuzu
1 tbsp. of maltose or rice syrup.
juice and rind of one orange (optional)

Mix the rice syrup with the rice cream and half fill separate dessert glasses; this will make 6 servings.

Bring water, salt, rice syrup and orange juice to a boil. Wash, halve and de-stone the fresh peaches; add these to the water and simmer for 3-5 minutes. Take out the peaches and peel off the skins which should come away easily. I do this partly because the colour of the peach beneath the skin is very beautiful. Place the peach with its centre upturned in the dessert glass, on top of the rice cream. Wash and blanch the cherries and place one of each of these inside the peach cup. At this point dilute kuzu with a little water and add to the cooking water. Add more sweetener if needed to your taste. Glaze the peach and cherry half with orange kuzu and chill this dessert for a little before serving.

GRILLED PEACHES WITH WALNUTS

3 ripe peaches
1/2 cup of chopped, roasted walnuts
2-3 tbsp. of currants
1 tbsp. tahini (brown)
1/2 tsp. miso

Soak the currants with a pinch of salt for 2-3 hours and chop them finely.

17

Wash, halve and de-stone the peaches. Grind half the walnuts in a suribachi and add the tahini and miso and a little water if necessary. Blend in the walnuts and currants and spoon this to fill the peach halves. Decorate with a walnut and put under the grill for 3-4 minutes. Serve immediately or chill.

STUFFED PEACHES

3 large peaches
1/2 cup of cous cous
1 cup of water
1 pinch of salt
3 tsp. rice syrup
1 tsp. of tahini
grated rind of 1 lemon
flaked almonds to decorate

Wash and steam cous cous in 1 cup of water for about 10 minutes with a pinch of salt. Combine cous cous, rice syrup, tahini and lemon rind and fill peach halves. Decorate with almonds and cook on gas 4 for about 20 minutes.

APPLE CUPS

4 large red apples
8 hunza apricots
1 pinch of salt
flaked almonds

Halve apples and scoop out to make cups. Boil the apples in a little water with a pinch of salt for about 2 minutes. Take the apples out and set them on small glass dishes. wash the apricots and using the apple cooking water, add more water if necessary to cover. Simmer the apricots for about an hour adding more water if necessary. Nearly all the cooking water should have been absorbed by the apricots when you have finished cooking them. Remove the apricot pits. Roast the flaked almonds, about 1 1/2 handfuls and when the apricots have cooled mix the almonds and apricots and fill the apple cups.

RED FRUIT DESSERT

1/2 lb mixed, fresh, red fruit
1 1/2 pts of water
2 tbsp. of kuzu
1 pinch of sea salt
2 tbsp. of rice syrup

Strawberries, raspberries or blackberries are perhaps the nicest fruits to choose, with cherries to decorate or as a shape contrast in the kuzu. Wash the fruit and leave it whole or slice half of it as you wish. Heat the water and salt, add the fruit and simmer for about 15 minutes. Dilute the kuzu and add this. add the rice syrup at the end of cooking as it loses its sweetness the more it is cooked. Serve in glass dessert dishes perhaps with some blanched fruit to garnish. This is a very simple, pretty dessert that can be made very quickly.

BLACKBERRY AND APRICOT PARFAIT

1/4 lb of blackberries
1 pt of water
1 pinch of sea salt
1 1/2 tbsp. of agar agar
1 tbsp. of kuzu
2 tbsp. of barley malt

12 hunza apricots

1 1/2 pts of water
1 pinch of salt
1 tbsp. of kuzu
1 1/2 tbsp. of agar agar
2 tbsp. of rice syrup.

Wash and simmer the hunza apricots in 1 1/2 pints of water with a pinch of salt for about an hour. Make sure you have roughly the same amount of water at the end as at the beginning by topping it up. Remove and de-pit the hunzas, meanwhile add the agar agar to the apricot cooking water. Put the hunzas back in the water and simmer for about 15 minutes. Dilute the kuzu and add this until a clear sauce is formed. Add the rice syrup and pour the apricots to half fill dessert glasses leaving the mixture to set for a while with the glass upright or on its side.

I prefer to pick wild blackberries just before making this dessert because they have such a sweet taste and a really clear energy of their own. wash the blackberries. Bring water and salt to a boil and add the blackberries and agar agar. add the barley malt and simmer for about 15 minutes, dilute the kuzu in a little cold water and add this to make a clear sauce. When the apricot agar agar has set   pour in the blackberries and leave to harden for about 2 hours before serving.

STRAWBERRY COUS COUS FLAN

3 cups of strawberries
2 cups of cous cous
6 cups of water
1 pinch of sea salt
juice and rind of one lemon
1/4 lb of walnuts
2 tbsp. of kuzu
2-3 tbsp. of rice syrup or barley malt

Wash and steam the cous cous for about 10 minutes with 4 cups of water and a pinch of salt. Scrub the skin of the lemon, grate the rind and add both the rind and juice to the cous cous. Roast and finely chop the walnuts and mix these in with the cous cous. This alone if put in a rinsed mould would make a nice cake, somewhat similar to madiera cake only of a wetter consistency. If lemon is too extreme for you to use because of the season or your condition, the cous cous base is delicious just with walnuts. To some people's taste a little sweetener is needed. Wet your hands and press the cous cous to about 1/3rd of an inch thickness into a large flan base.

Wash and slice the strawberries. Heat 2 cups of water with a pinch of salt and simmer the strawberries for a few minutes. It is nice to leave a few strawberries whole to add to the decorative effect. Arrange the strawberries on top of the cous cous. Add diluted kuzu to the strawberry cooking water and when the kuzu has become clear add the barley malt or rice syrup. Barley malt has a tendency to make the binding effect of kuzu less strong as barley malt has a more yin, expansive effect than rice syrup, so you may have to add a little more kuzu to compensate, if you are using barley malt.
   Variations; Almost any fruit is nice on this cous cous base, also a mixture of fruit and nuts would be delicious and decoratively effective, for instance red apple half-moons and whole roasted walnuts; peach halves with a raspberry kuzu sauce is very pretty.

STEAMED COUS COUS CAKE

1 cup of raisins
1 cup of dried apricots
6 cups of apple juice
3 cups of cous cous

3/4 tsp. of sea salt
1/2 cup of corn oil
1 tsp. of freshly grated ginger juice
1 tsp. grated lemon rind (optional)

Wash and soak all the dried fruit in apple juice overnight. Mix dry
ingredients together and rub in oil and ginger juice. Heat apple juice and
fruit until they are nearly boiling and add them to the dry ingredients.
Stir gently until the cous cous begins to expand and the mixture becomes
thick but still pourable.

Pour mixture into a mould and cover it tightly with foil. Put 1 1/2 " of
water into a pot large enough to put the mould into, put the mould in and
cover the pan with a lid. Make sure no water or steam reaches the cake.
Steam the cous cous cake on a medium flame for about 1/2 an hour. Let the
cake cool thoroughly before slicing it. This cake is moist and of a
pudding-like consistency.

ORANGE CUSTARD

1 cup of apple juice
1 cup of rice syrup
1 tsp. grated orange rind
1 tsp. of grated ginger juice (optional)
1/4 tsp. sea salt
2 cups of orange juice
3 cups of water
3 tbsp. of agar agar
2 1/2 tbsp. of kuzu.

Bring water, apple juice, salt and agar agar to a boil and simmer them for
10 minutes. Add the orngc rind and ginger juice and simmer for 5 more
minutes. Dilute the kuzu in the orange juice and stir the kuzu in so that
it mixes evenly, cook for a few minutes more and pour the custard into a
bowl. Let the custard cool and just before it sets whip it with a hand
whisk. Let the custard cool completely before serving it. Roast almonds
can make a good garnish. You may find that you have to vary the amounts of
kuzu and agar agar to find the consistency which you really like.

BAKED SPICED PEARS

6 ripe pears
3 tbsp. of barley malt
3 tbsp of water
1-2 tsp. of ginger juice

Wash the pears and place them so that they are standing upright on a
baking tray. Pre-heat the oven to gas 5 or 6. Heat barley malt and water
in a saucepan and pour this over each per to cover. Place the pears in the
oven for 20-30 minutes. Grate the fresh ginger root and squeeze out the
juice with your hand. Pour a little of this juice lightly over the pears
and either cook them for a couple of minutes longer or serve them as they
are.
       Variations: This recipe works well with apples also.

BAKED APPLES

Wash apples and bake them at gas 5 for about 20 minutes. Baking apples can
also be cored and various nut and fruit fillings can be added. We always
use eating apples for baking because their natural sweetness means that
thay do not require the addition of any other sweetener, also their
natural sweetness means that they are less acidic than cooking apples.
Ripe apples are generally yellow or red skinned and there is no sourness
in their flavour.

Raisins which have been soaked for a couple of hours with a pinch of salt
add to the sweetness of the apple if they are pressed down the centre of
the apple before baking. Miso and tahini spread is also delicious if mixed
with currants and put in the centre of a cored apple before baking. To
make the spread:- roughly 3 teaspoons of tahini to 1 teaspoon of miso and
1 or 2 teaspoons of water to blend to the right consistency. For a lighter
taste the apple can be cored and then baked plain and a strawberry,
blackberry or apricot kuzu sauce poured over it at the end. Walnuts, lemon
rind and miso can also make a tasty filling for baked apples.

APPLE CUSTARD

3 cups of apple juice
1 pinch of sea salt
2 tbsp. of sesame butter (dark)
3 fresh apples, cored and thinly sliced
2 tbsp. of kuzu
1/2 cup of cold water

Heat the apple juice. There are two types of sesame butter designated as
light and dark. The difference is that the darker of the sesame butters
has been roasted which makes it more digestible than the light sesame
butter and so I generally prefer to use the dark sesame butter in making
desserts particularly if it isn´t going to be cooked. Dilute the sesame
butter in a little hot apple juice by creaming it in a suribacni. Add
apple slices to the apple juice together with the salt and simmer until
the apples are soft and mushy. Dilute kuzu in 1/2 cup of cold water and
add to the mixture. Simmer until custard is thick and clear, and add this
slowly to the sesame butter in the suribachi.. Place in a serving bowl and
allow the custard to cool for a few hours before serving.
       Variations:- Other fruits could be used to make a different kind of
custard such as hunza apricots which need a longer cooking time, but are
delicious. A similar custard can be made with raisins or sultanas which
have been pureed but the colour is not so attractive. A finer and smoother
custard can be made by ommitting the fruit altogether and just adding
another tablespoon of sesame butter for a very creamy taste.

STRAWBERRY MOUSSE

3 cups of fresh strawberries
1 pinch of sea salt
1 1/2 tbsp. of agar flakes
2 cups of rice cream
3 cups of apple juice
2 tbsp. of sesame butter

Wash and slice the strawberries leaving one or two whole for garnishing; set them aside. Place apple juice, agar and salt in a saucepan and simmer for 15 minutes, stirring occasionally. Turn off the flame and add the strawberries. Blend the rice cream, sesame butter and agar agar in a blender or with a hand whisk and chill until set in a mould or individual dessert glasses.

WHIPPED RAISIN MOUSSE

2 cups of alexia raisins
6 cups of water
1 pinch of sea salt
4 tbsp. of agar flakes
1 cup of sunflower or sesame seeds

Simmer the raisins with the water, salt and agar agar for 20-30 minutes. Pour the mixture into a mould and allow it to cool and gel but not set hard. Wash, sort and dry roast sesame seeds or sunflower seeds. If using sesame seeds grind these in a suribachi until they are at least 50% ground. Whip the raisin mould and the sesame or sunflower seeds together in a blender and either place in individual dessert glasses or a serving bowl with a garnish of nuts, seeds or seasonal flowers.
    Variations: Apple or apricot can both be used to make a delicious whipped mousse.

KANTEN

Kanten is a very simple dessert which we quite frequently make. It is a complete and really delicious and nutritious substitute for jellies made in the conventional way and has infinite possibilities for variation. Kanten is made using agar agar which is a seaweed gelatine, a blend of six different seaweeds. It is high in minerals and makes an excellent natural laxative. Kanten is cooling for the body and is particularly appropriate for women and for the summer heat. It is a light, refreshing dessert and the use of agar agar increases the digestibility of the fruit. The simplest form of kanten is fresh or dried fruit cooked for 15-20 minutes with agar agar and a pinch of salt. This can be made sweeter by the addition of grain sweeteners or richer by the addition of seeds and nuts. Agar agar comes in various forms; older cooking books refer to blocks of agar agar, these I have never seen. Usually agar agar comes in the form of flakes, occasionally as powder. If you are using flakes, about 3 tablespoons to a pint of water is a fairly accurate measurement; if you are using powder you will need about half this amount.

DANDELION COFFEE AND APPLE KUZU KANTEN

1 1/2 pints of water
3 teaspoons of dandelion coffee
1 cup of dried apple rings
1/2 cup of walnuts
3 tablespoons of agar flakes
1 pinch of salt

Bring water to the boil and add the dandelion coffee. Simmer this for 15-20 minutes and strain off the dandelion root. Add enough water to make 1 1/2 pints again and add agar agar, salt and dried apple. Simmer these together for 25- 30 minutes. Meanwhile dry roast the walnuts and either chop them very finely (leaving a few whole for garnish) or grind them to a paste in a suribachi. Add them to the kanten. If they are in paste form the kanten juice will have to be added slowly to the walnut paste until a light cream is formed. This cream can be added to the kanten. Rinse a mould and decorate the bottom of the mould with a few whole roasted walnuts. On top of the walnuts place a few apple rings, and on top of this slowly and gently pour in the kanten mixture. Allow the kanten to set firm which takes 2-3 hours and turn it out of the mould to serve.

MELON AND RASPBERRY BOATS

1 melon (honeydew or cassava)
1 large punnet of raspberries
1 pinch of salt
1 pint of water
1 tbsp. of kuzu
3 tbsp. of agr flakes
2 tbsp of rice syrup.

Wash and halve the melon. Remove the seeds and scoop out some of the melon to make a good deep cup shape. Save the scooped melon for a fruit salad. If necessary cut a slice from the bottom of the melon so that the melon stands firmly. Puncture the inside of the melon ith a chopstick or similarly shaped utensil; this helps the raspberry jelly to adhere to the surface of the melon.

Bring water, salt, agar agar and raspberries to a boil and simmer for about 10 minutes. Add the kuzu diluted in a little cold water and simmer for another five minutes. Remove from the flame and stir in the rice syrup. Pour the raspberry kanten into the melon cups and leave to set for about 3 hours. To serve cut into boat or half-moon wedges. It is good to use a fruit in the kanten that creates an interesting colour contrast with the melon, such as red fruits:- strawberries, raspberries or blackberries, or orange fruits:- peaches or apricots or a mixture of colours such as pear and cherry. The kanten mixture has to be made quite firm to adhere to the melon.

WATERMELON COMPOTE

1 water melon
1/4 teaspoon of sea salt
5 cups of water
3 tbsp. of kuzu
1/2 lb of fresh strawberries
2 ripe peaches
6 cherries
juice and rind of 1 orange (optional)

Cut the water melon in half, de-seed it and take out the pulp. Simmer the pulp with 2 cups of water and half of the slt for about 40 minuts. This makes a sweet syrup. Add two cups of water to the syrup with the orange juice and rind. Wash and slice the strawberries and add these. Mix the kuzu with a little cold water and add this to the mixture. simmer for a couple of minutes and pour into the water melon halves.

Boil remaining cup of water with a pinch of salt. Wash and halve peaches, simmer them for a couple of minutes, remove and slice. Simmer cherries for a couple of minutes and use these with the peach slices for garnish.

24

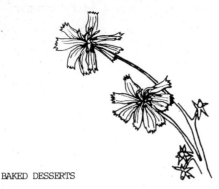

BAKED DESSERTS

Baking is just about the most contractive and heavy style of cooking available to us and tends to create a heavy, stagnating energy in the person who eats a lot of baked foods, particularly if the baking is combined with the use of flour in cooking. The use of baked desserts is most appropriate to the winter because of the very warming nature of this method of cooking, baking is also much more appropriate for someone who is physically active otherwise excessive energy is easily gathered in the body, which has a tendency to become blocked and cause stagnation in the activity of our body´s organs, particularly the intestines. This physical stagnation has a direct correlation with and effect upon our mental and emotional activity and attitudes.

Baking, particularly the combination of flour and oil is used excessively in the conventional western diet and has a detrimental effect on our clarity of thought, our physical well-being and our emotional responsiveness. However- despite these facts many of us have a craving for this kind of food and so I have incorporated in this section, recipes which use the minimum of flour and yet can still satisfy the baked quality we are used to in desserts.

LEMON MILLET CAKE

1 cup of whole, hulled millet
3 cups of water
1 cup of alexia raisins
3 tablespoons barley malt or rice syrup
2 cups of cooked cous cous
1/2 tsp. of sea salt
rind and juice of two lemons
1/2 a cup of roast sunflower seeds
oil to grease cake tin

Wash the millet in a sieve and dry roast it in a frying pan until it releases a nutty fragrance. Meanwhile bring the 3 cups of water, salt and raisins to a boil and add the millet. Turn the flame to very low and placing the lid on leave the millet undisturbed for 30-40 minutes until it is cooked. Take the millet off the heat and add the barley malt, lemon and cous cous together with the sunflower seeds. Place the mixture in two cake tins and put in a pre-heated oven at regulo 5 for about 50 minutes.

Take the cake out and allow it to cool before turning the cake out of the cake tin. For a more traditional finish to the cake, choose a glaze or icing from that section of the book and make a sandwich cake with nuts or fruits as garnish.

CARROT CAKE

1 lb of grated carrots
1/2 cup of chestnut puree
3 tbsp. of soya flour
3 tbsp. of brown rice flour
1 cup of any cooked grain
2 tbsp. of corn oil
1 cup of water
1/4 tsp. of sea salt

2 tsp. of fresh ginger juice

Mix all ingredients together and pour into a shallow cake tin. Bake at regulo 5 for 45 minutes covered and a further 20 minutes uncovered. Take out, allow to cool, turn the cake out and serve it. A nice icing for this cake is a simple barley malt kuzu glaze made with pureed raisins and walnuts to garnish.

Variations:- For a sweeter taste in the basic recipe you can add about a 1/2 cup of raisins or currants. This cake could be steamed in a pressure cooker for 1 1/4 hours as long as it is prepared like the christmas pudding i.e carefully sealed.

APPLE AND APRICOT COUS COUS CAKE

2 cups of cooked cous cous
1 1/2 dried apple rings
1/2 cup of whole apricots
3/4 cup of water
2 pinches of sea slt
2 tbsp. of rice syrup or barley malt

Wash the apples and apricots and simmer them with water and a pinch of salt for 20-30 minutes, until all the water is absorbed. Mix the fruit with the cous cous, together with the sweetener and put this mixture in a cake dish. Cover the cake dish with foil so that moisture isn't lost and allow to cool.

Variations:- fresh fruit can be used instead of dried. Lemon peel and lemon juice or ginger juice can be added to give a different flavour to this dessert. Roasted nuts and seeds add a lovely crunchy texture.

APPLE STRUDEL

4 fresh apples
1 tbsp. of barley malt
1 cup of chopped walnuts
 1 pinch of sea salt

1/2 a cup of water

Wash, de-core and slice the apples into half-moons. Simmer the apples, salt, barley malt and wate until all the water has been absorbed. Roast and chop the walnuts. Allow the apples and walnuts to cool, mix them together and set them aside.

2 cups of oatflakes
1 cup of w/w pastry flour
6 tbsp. of corn oil
 pinch of sea salt
cold water to mix

Mix all ingredients using as little water as possible to make a dough consistency. Leave the dough in the fridge or other cool place for an hour or more. Roll the pastry out between two pieces of greaseproof paper as this allows for a thinner pastry. Spread the apple and walnut evenly over the pastry and roll into a log folding in the ends to prevent the filling from coming out. Bake at reg. 6 for 30 minutes and after baking slice the strudel. For a shiny top, glaze the strudel with heated barley malt about 2 minutes before taking it out, this will also give a slightly toffeeish taste and texture.
    Variations:- You can use almost any combination of fruits and nuts, either fresh, seasonal ones or dried ones. Around christmas time a chestnut and raisin strudel or a mincemeat strudel is a really nice addition to the store of christmas goodies.

cookies

There are many, many excellent recipes for cookies if you are happy using flour, so I thought I´d just include one possibility that excludes the use of flour.

2 cups of oatflakes
water to mix
2 pinches of salt
1/2 cup of raisins
1/4 - 1/2 cup of hazlenuts

Soak the raisins with a pinch of salt and just enough water to cover for about 2 hours. Drain off the soaking water and use this to mix with the oatflakes to make a paste. Mix in the raisins and hazlenuts and place on an oiled baking tray. Cook in a pre-heated medium oven for about 30 minutes. Be careful to check them from about 20 minutes on.
    Variations:- Using oatmeal, rice flour or a little oil in the cookies will make a crunchier and richer taste. If you are using oil then 1 tablespoon of oil, preferably corn oil, to 3 cups of oats or flour is a standard measure. For extra sweetness barley malt or rice syrup can be added. Sometimes umeboshi paste is a tasty substitute for salt giving the cookies a more tangy flavour. Ginger juice can be added, lemon rind, grated carrot or shiso leaves for different flavours.

3 fresh red apples
1 cup apple juice
1/2 tbsp. of kuzu
1 pinch of sea salt

1 1/2 cups of pastry flour
1/4 cup of corn oil
1 pinch of salt
a little ginger juice

cold water to mix.Wash, de-core and slice the apples into half-moons.
Bring the apples to a boil in the apple juice with a pinch of salt. Dilute
the kuzu in a little water and add this to make a thick sauce around the
apples and set aside.
Mix the flour and oil, as little cold water as possible, a pinch of salt
and a little ginger juice to make a dough consistency. Set the dough aside
for an hour in a cool place. Roll the pastry out between two pieces of
greaseproof paper so the pastry can be made thinner without it breaking or
sticking. Oil the bottom of a pastry dish and layer in pastry with the
apple kuzu between. Bake in a medium oven for about 30 minutes.

FRUIT AND NUT BARS

1 cup of diced apple
1 cup of chopped walnuts
1/2 cup of chopped almonds
1 cup of currants
2 cups of rolled oats (medium)
1/2 cup of whole wheat flour
4 cups of apple juice
3/4 tsp. of sea salt

Soak the currants in a cup of apple juice and a little salt for 2 hours.
Wash and dice the apple and mix together all the ingredients. A thick
batter should be formed which still adheres to a spoon when it is turned
upside down. Bake in a medium oven for 45- 50 minutes after spreading the
mixture onto an oiled baking tray. Allow to cool and cut into slices.

SUMMER PUDDING

1 1/2 lbs of fresh fruit (traditionally red fruit)
1 cup of rice syrup
1 cup of water
1 pinch of sea salt
6-8 slices of wholewheat bread

Wash and slice the fruit. Simmer the fruit with water and salt for about
5 minutes and add rice syrup at the end of cooking. Line a glass bowl with
bread, cutting it to make sure that there are no gaps. Spoon in fruit and
fruit juice so that it holds bread in place. Cover with a small plate that
is weighted down to press on the bread and chill overnight. Turn out and
serve. This pudding needs at lest 10 hours to acquire the right
consistency. It is a very traditional english pudding.

NOODLE KUGEL

3 cups of wholewheat noodles
1 cup of raisins
7 cups of water
3 tbsp. of barley malt
2 tbsp. of tahini
2 pinches of salt divided

Bring 6 cups of water to a boil with a pinch of salt, add the noodles and simmer until these are 3/4 cooked (7-10 minutes). Remove and drain, saving the cooking water. Add the raisins to the cooking water with the other pinch of salt and simmer them for about 20 minutes. Mix the tahini in a suribachi to a cream by slowly adding the last cup of water to it.

Combine all these ingredients together with the barley malt in a casserole dish and bake in a medium pre-heated oven for about 20 minutes. Noodle kugel can be served warm or chilled.
    Variations:- You can include other dried fruit in this recipe such as apricots; also mix in or sprinkle with roast almonds or walnuts before serving. A touch of lemon or ginger juice is an interesting addition. Occasionally, for a more sensorial summer dish a little sugar free soya milk could be added before baking. Soya milk is very yin and pretty indigestible, so it is good to boil the milk with a strip of kombu for a few minutes before adding it to the noodle kugel. Cooking with kombu helps balance the high fat and protein content of the soya milk. However, even prepared this way, soya milk is quite extreme and should be regarded as a treat rather than a usual ingredient of macrobiotic desserts.

APPLE CRUNCH

1 cup of dried apples
1 cup of fresh red apples half-moons.
3 cups of water
1 pinch of salt
1 tbsp. of kuzu.

2 cups of rolled oats
1 cup of chopped walnuts
1 cup of granola
1 tbsp. of barley malt
1 tbsp. of corn oil (optional)

Wash and slice the apples. Combine with water and salt and simmer for at least 20 minutes. Dilute the kuzu in cold water and add this to make a sauce. Pour the apple kuzu into a glass baking dish so that the dish is half full.

Mix the oats and oil by hand. Add the granola, chopped nuts and barley malt and cover the apple kuzu. Bake in a medium oven 20-30 minutes and serve hot or cold. We like to serve this dish with a tofu cream which is made thus:-
Steam tofu for 10 minutes. Sort, wash and dry roast sesame seeds then grind them finely in a suribachi. Add the tofu and a tiny bit of miso or umeboshi paste, just enough to balance out the yin of the tofu but not make the crem too salty. Mix these ingredients well and serve them on the apple crunch. The juxta position of sweet dessert and creamy slightly salty topping is very interesting, if not entirely conventional.

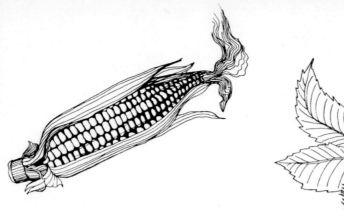

DESSERTS FROM BEANS, NUTS AND VEGETABLES.

Many different and delicious desserts can be made using beans, nuts, seeds and vegetables, sometimes with the addition of a little fruit or fruit juice but often on their own. Chestnuts, for example can make a very sweet and satisfyng dessert which is of a totally different quality to a fruit dessert. This kind of dessert will be especially appropriate for many people who are trying to improve their health particularly if their health problems have arisen because the person is overly yin.

ADUKI BEAN DESSERTS

Traditionally, in Japan, many desserts are made using aduki beans, and we have borrowed a few of their simpler recipes which we use quite often. Desserts made with aduki beans, particularly when combined with either pumpkin or chestnuts, make a sweet tasting and quite strengthening dessert.

ADUKI AND CHESTNUT BALLS

1 cup of aduki beans
1 cup of chestnuts
6 cups of water
1 7" strip of kombu
1 1/2 tsp. of shoyu

Wash the aduki beans and the dried chestnuts and soak them for between two and four hours; the longer the beans and chestnuts are soaked the shorter the length of cooking time they will need. Wipe the salt from the kombu with a clean, damp cloth and place this at the bottom of a cooking pot, add the adukis, chestnuts and water and simmer them together for about an hour and 20 minutes. At this point the kombu can be removed if you do not want it in your dessert; otherwise the kombu disintegrates and blends harmoniously with the adukis and chestnuts. We use kombu to provide a mineral balance to the high protein and fat content of beans which aids digestibility. At this point when the beans and chestnuts are 80% cooked add the shoyu and simmer until the adukis and chestnuts are very soft and mash easily. At the end of cooking the water should be absorbed but the beans should not be dry.

Transfer the adukis and chestnuts to a suribachi and mash them to a paste before making them into little bite sized balls. These balls can be further decorated by rolling them in roast, ground sesame seeds, flaked almonds or slithers of ginger candy. For an interesting colour contrast the adukis and chestnuts can be cooked separately and used to wrap around each other to make a twi-coloured ball which can then be halved and decorated with hazlenuts, almonds or walnuts.

30

Variations:- In the same way twi-coloured balls can be made with pumpkin and aduki beans cooked separately. Onion butter (made by pressure cooking onion quarters for 40 minutes in very little water, then seasoning with umeboshi and miso) can also be used if it is thickened a little with agar agar. Ginger is a really tasty additional seasoning to this dessert.

For a sweeter dessert the aduki beans can be cooked with raisins and perhaps a little barley malt added at the end of cooking. Chestnuts and hunza apricots make a very sweet dessert either as a puree garnished with roast almonds or as chestnut balls.

ADUKI BEAN AND CHESTNUT KANTEN

Using the same ingredients as the above recipe just use 2-3 extra cups of water and two tablespoons of agar agar added about 20 minutes before the end of cooking. Pour the kanten into a rinsed mould and allow about 2 hours for it to set. Kanten is especially delicious lightly chilled. This makes a more cooling dessert than the chestnut and aduki balls and so is more appropriate for summer or an overly yang condition. Orange juice and orange rind can be added near the end of cooking to add more sparkle to the dessert. The same variations in combining ingredients for making the kanten are appropriate here as they are for the aduki and chestnut ball recipe above.

CHESTNUT DESSERT

2 cups of chestnuts
6 cups of water
2 pinches of salt
1 7" strip of kombu
2 oranges, rind and juice.

Wash and soak chestnuts for between 2 and 4 hours and cook them with water and kombu for 1 1/2 hours. Remove the kombu, season with sea salt and simmer for about 30 minutes more, adding more water if necessary. At the end of cooking there should be about 2 cups of water left. Sieve out the chestnuts and puree these in the suribachi. Grate the orange rind and squeeze the juice into the remaining chestnut water. Add the pureed chestnut and simmer for a few minutes to allow the orange flavour to blend with the chestnuts. If necessary add a little kuzu to thicken the dessert to a custard consistency. Garnish with rounds of orange and serve hot or chilled.

Variations. This chestnut dessert is a very strong sweet taste and really needs another flavour to give the dish life and movement, hence the addition of tangy orange. If this is too extreme for you the addition of a bitter or pungent flavour would be equally as effective in making a more dynamic dessert. Walnuts or roast, ground sesame seeds will give an interesting bitter contrast to the sweetness of the chestnuts and ginger or a garnish of lemon will add a pungent or sour quality to the dessert.

PUMPKIN DESSERT

2 cups of Hokkaido or similar pumpkin
1 cup of raisins
2 red dessert apples
2 cups of water
3 pinches of salt
1 tbsp of kuzu
1 tbsp. barley malt or rice syrup.

Wash and slice the pumpkin finely. Pressure cook the pumpkin with the raisins, 2 pinches of salt and one cup of water for 20 minutes then puree them in a suribachi. Place in a baking tray and bake in a medium oven for 30-40 minutes. Take out and allow to cool.

Wash and slice the apples into half-moons. Blanch these in 1 cup of water together with a pinch of salt. Sieve out the apples and decorate the pumpkin dessert. Using the apple cooking water, add the kuzu and sweetener, and make a glaze to pour over the apples. Allow the whole dessert to cool for about 2 hours and serve in slices.

CHESTNUT KINTON

1 cup of onion puree
2 cups of pumpkin puree
2 cups of chestnut puree

Mix all the ingredients together and place them in a rinsed mould. Allow the dessert to cool and cut it into squares or triangles to serve with a nut garnish.

Variations:- Apple puree could be substituted for the onions if desired and ginger juice gives a really delicious flavour. A little agar agar could be added to the purees. Layer one puree in a rinsed mould and allow it to harden slightly; pour in the next layer and allow this to harden slightly. Swirl the two layers together to make an interesting pattern and pour in the top layer. Swirl again, this time delicately and leave the kanten to set before serving.

COFFEE KUZU KANTEN

1 1/2 pints of water
3 tbsp. of dandelion coffee
3 tbsp. of agar agar
1 pinch of sea salt
1 tbsp. of kuzu
2 tbsp. of tahini (dark).
1 tbsp. of barley malt

Simmer dandelion coffee in the water for about 15 minutes, put it through a sieve and save the coffee to use again. Add agar agar, barley malt,and sea salt. Simmer for a further 15 minutes; dilute the kuzu in cold water and stir this in gently. Place the tahini in a suribachi and dilute it to a cream with a little cold water. Slowly mix the dandelion coffee kanten with the sesame cream. Pour into a rinsed mould and allow to set. Decorate with roasted walnuts.

COFFEE MOUSSE

1 pt. of apple juice
3 tbsp. of agar agar flakes
2 tbsp. of grain coffee (barleycup)
1 pinch of sea salt
1 tbsp. of tahini
1 tbsp. of rice syrup (optional)
roasted almonds.

Simmer the apple juice together with the agar agar and sea salt for ten minutes. Dilute grain coffee in a little water and add this to the apple juice. Cook the mixture for 10 minutes more and then allow it to cool until it has hardened. Place the kanten in a blender and mix with tahini, adding a little rice syrup for a sweeter taste.

For a slightly better quality dessert sort, roast and grind your own sesame seeds. This makes a less oily and more digestible dessert. Pour the mousse into individual dessert glasses and serve with a garnish of chopped roast almonds.

COFFEE CARAGEEN MOULD

4 cups of oat milk
25 gr. of carageen moss
3 tsp. of grain coffee
2-3 tbsp. of rice syrup or barley malt.

Wash the moss and soak it for an hour. Drain the carageen and simmer it with the oat milk very gently until the milk begins to thicken and coats the back of a spoon; this should be about 20 minutes. Add grain coffee and rice syrup. Pour into a rinsed mould and allow to set. Turn out and serve.

SESAME KUZU SQUARES.

1 cup of sesame seeds
1 cup of kuzu
7 cups of water
1 pinch of sea salt
2 tbsp. of rice syrup.

Sort, wash, dry roast and grind the sesame seeds. These need sorting as they often contain mouse droppings and twigs. Grind the seeds very well until they are almost paste-like in consistency. Bring the water to a boil; use some of this water to mix the sesame seeds to a thin cream. Pour this cream back into the water. You can either use all the sesame seeds or, if you want a smoother textured dessert, pour the sesame seeds through a sieve. Simmer on a low flame. Dilute the kuzu with cold water, making sure there are no lumps in it. Take the water and seeds off the flame and add the sea salt and kuzu, stirring sothat the kuzu mixes evenly. Put the mixture back on a low flame for a few minutes. When it has finished cooking add the rice syrup and pour the sesame kuzu into a mould to set. When it is thoroughly cool, cut into little squares or triangles and serve.

CARROT MACAROONS

1 cup of whole oats
1 pinch of sea salt
3 cups of water
3/4 cup of grated carrot
3 tbsp. of peanut butter

Wash and soak the oats in one cup of water for at least 4 to six hours. Pressure cook the oats with the additional two cups of water and a pinch of salt for 1 - 1 1/4 hours. Mix in the carrots and peanut butter and if the mixture is too wet a little rice flour. Spoon the mixture onto a cookie sheet and bake at regulo 5 for 50 minutes. These macaroons store best if kept cool.

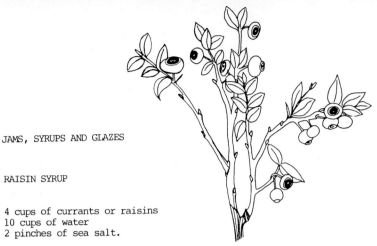

JAMS, SYRUPS AND GLAZES

RAISIN SYRUP

4 cups of currants or raisins
10 cups of water
2 pinches of sea salt.

Bring currants, water and salt to a boil in a large heavy saucepan. Lower the flame, cover and simmer for 1 1/2 hours. The syrup can be drained from the fruit pulp and used as a sweetener in an other wise plain kanten. This juice could also be thickened with a little kuzu and used as a semi-clear cake topping. Almonds or walnuts could be roasted, chopped and added to the syrup as a cake filling.

Alternatively the juice and fruit pulp could be pureed together in a suribachi and used as a jam.

PUREED CHESTNUTS

2 cups of dried chestnuts (1 1/2 lbs fresh chestnuts)
water
2 pinches of sea salt

Either soak the dried chestnuts for 3 hours or dry roast them for 10 minutes or so in the oven. Boil the chestnuts with one 7" strip of kombu which has been wiped clean of excess salt, and water to cover. Make sure you use the chestnut soaking water as this is very flavoursome; add more water as the chestnuts continue to cook. After about an hour remove the kombu and add salt. Simmer until the chestnuts are very soft and mash esily, about 40 minutes to one hour further cooking time. At the end of cooking a little water should be left to make a puree consistency. Mash the chestnuts in a suribachi (a Japanese pestle and mortar)and mix with the remaining cooking water to the desired consistency. This can be used as a delicious cake icing because it is so naturally sweet. Ginger juice adds a lot of zest to chestnut puree.

If you are using fresh chestnuts, wash them and cut a slit in their skin. Bake in a pre-heated 350 degree oven for 30 minutes or until the chestnuts are soft. The chestnuts can be tested for softness by removing one and peeling it; the chestnut should pierce easily with a fork. Let the chestnuts cool before mashing them. Heat a little water with a pinch of salt and mix this with the chestnuts until the desired consistency is reached. Chestnut puree makes a lovely filling for individual tart cases particularly with ginger candy or a barley malt glace cherry.

Variations:- CHESTNUT CREAM FILLING

            2 cups of cooked chestnuts
            2 tbsp. of rice syrup

2 tsp. lemon juice
1 tsp. of lemon rind
1 pinch of sea salt

Puree the cooked chestnuts with some of the remaining cooking water to the desired consistency and blend with the rest of the ingredients, dry roasting the sea salt briefly in a frying pan first. For a creamier consistency a little tahini can be added.

APPLE SAUCE

6 cups of sweet apples
1 1/2 cups of water
Juice and grated rind of one lemon (optional)
1/4 tsp. of sea salt

Wash, core and slice apples. Simmer with water and salt in a heavy saucepan for 30-40 minutes, stirring occasionally to prevent burning. Red apples give the sauce a lovely rose pink colour. Add the lemon juice and rind about 10 minutes before the end of cooking, this adds a lovely tang to the sauce.

Variations:- For those with a sweet tooth a little barley malt or rice syrup could be added. Instead of lemon, ginger juice adds an interesting sparkle. Raisins can be added to make a sweeter sauce. This sauce can be used as a jam, a cake filling, a filling for individual pastry cases or as a sauce to pour over a simple steamed cous cous pudding e.t.c.

APPLE BUTTER

Puree apple sauce and cook it in a heavy lidded saucepan to about 1/2 its volume, stirring occasionally to prevent burning. When ready the apple butter will be quite dark in colour.

ALMOND BUTTER.

3 cups of whole almonds
1/4 tsp. of sea salt

Roast the almonds in a medium oven for 15-20 minutes, stirring them occasionally. Grind the almonds in a grain mill to a fine paste. Dry roast the salt in a pan for a couple of minutes and blend with the almond paste.

Variations:- almond or any other nut or seed butter can be mixed in a suribachi to make a runny cream consistency and this can be used as a rich sauce for fruit crumbles and grain desserts.

SESAME BUTTER

3 cups of whole sesame seeds
1/4 tsp. of sea salt

Sort and wash the sesame seeds and dry roast them in a skillet until the seeds crush easily when rubbed between the first and third fingers. If the flame is too high the seeds will pop and jump out of the pan and also tend to burn easily, a medium-low flame is best. For what to do next, follow the recipe for making almond butter.
Variations:- sunflower seed butter can be made in a similar way.

RASPBERRY OR MELBA SAUCE

4 oz. of fresh raspberries
1 tbsp. of mirin
2 tbsp. of rice syrup
1 pinch of sea salt
1/4 pint of water

Wash and chop the raspberries. Simmer them with the water and salt until the water is almost gone, add rice syrup and mirin and turn off heat. Puree the sauce in a suribachi and pour it over a grain dessert such as an oatflake mould.

AMASAKE ICING

2 cups of pureed amasake
2 tsp. agar agar flakes
1 tsp. of grated lemon peel
1/2 cup of water
1/4 tsp. of sea salt

Bring the water and agar agar to a boil and simmer for 15 minutes with the sea salt. Add the amasake and the lemon peel and cook a few minutes more. Remove the icing from the heat and allow it to set. Whip the icing with a hand whisk or blender into a cream and spread onto a cake or pudding.
Variations:- A little orange juice, ginger juice or vanilla extract could be added to give a different flavoured icing. A couple of teaspoons of grain coffee such as barley cup will give an interesting coffee icing.

OAT MILK ICING

2 cups of oat milk
1 cup of apple juice
2 tsp. of grated lemon rind

2 tsp. of grated lemon rind

2 tsp. of lemon juice
1 tbsp. of rice syrup
1 pinch of sea salt
1/4 cup of kuzu

To make the oat milk; pressure cook 1 cup of oats which have been washed with 4 cups of water for 1 1/4 hours. Strain off the liquid and save the oats for breakfast cereal or soup.

Blend all the other ingredients together except for the kuzu and simmer with the oat milk for 15-20 minutes. Dilute the kuzu in as little water as possible and add this to the oat milk, simmer for a few minutes more. Allow the mixture to cool and whip it into a creamy consistency with a hand whisk or blender. This makes a tasty dessert as it is, a rich cream topping for a fruit tart or a good cake icing.

APRICOT SPREAD

1/2 lb of dried apricots
apple juice to cover
1 tbsp. of kuzu
2 pinches of sea salt

Simmer the apricots with juice and salt until they are soft. Puree the apricots in a foodmill or blender. Dissolve the kuzu in a little water and pour the puree and kuzu back into the saucepan, stirring to mix them. Simmer the apricots until the mixture thickens and use as a spread for a cous cous or millet cake or over bread, crackers or rice cakes.

OAT CREAM

1 cup of rolled oats
4 cups of water
1 pinch of sea salt
4 tbsp. of rice syrup
1 tbsp. of tahini (optional)

Cook the oats, water and salt as you would for porridge, making sure you simmer the oats for at least 20-30 minutes. Add rice syrup and tahini, adjust the liquid to the desired consistency and blend the ingredients in a blender. With tahini this oat cream will be pretty mucous forming but if it is for special occasions and the added richness appeals, it is fine to use.
    Variation:- A couple of teaspoons of grain coffee could be added to the oat cream before it is cooked to make a coffee cream. Oat cream can be used as a cake filling or icing, especially with the addition of some chopped roast nuts.

GINGER CANDY

ginger

rice syrup

Wash fresh ginger and cut it into very thin slithers. Remove the skin and simmer the ginger in a little water and a pinch of salt for a few minutes. Remove this water and save it for using in another dish. Simmer the ginger pieces in a little fresh water, add rice syrup, maltose or barley malt and simmer on a low flame for about 10 minutes. All the water should be absorbed. Spread the pieces of ginger out to dry on a flat plate or baking sheet. You can cut the pieces of ginger into whatever shapes you like before you start cooking with them, the prettier the shapes the more appealing the ginger will be when used for a garnish.

CANDIED ALMONDS.

almonds
barley malt

Heat enough barley malt in a pan to cover the amount of nuts you wish to use. The barley malt has to be really hot and ideally when it is dropped into cold water it should harden slightly. When the malt is hot, dip the almonds in and place them on an oiled baking tray. The oil is necessary so that the malt doesn't stick to the tray. Put the nuts in a medium pre-heated oven for 3-5 minutes, being careful that the malt does not burn. Take the nuts out and allow them to cool. These make a lovely party snack and are ideal for garnish.

   Variations:- Cherries are excellent candied, keep their stalks on as this helps when you are dipping them in the malt.

CHRISTMAS COOKING

MINCE PIES

Mincemeat

5 cups of apples
2-3 cups of currants or raisins
1 1/2 cups of apple juice or water
grated rind and juice of 1 orange
rind of 1/2 a lemon
1 tsp. of ginger juice
cinnamon (optional),
1 pinch of sea salt
2 tsp. of miso (either barley or hatcho)
1 cup of finely chopped walnuts

Wash, core and slice the apples. Simmer them with the apple juice and a
pinch of salt   until they make a sauce conistency, about 30-40 minutes.
The raisins should be soaked overnight with a pinch of salt to bring out
their sweetness; they can be added to the apples at this stage. Add all
the other ingredients except the miso and walnuts. Puree the miso in a
little water and stir it into the mixture. When the mincemeat is a fairly
thick consistency take it off the heat. Dry roast the walnuts and chop
them finely. Stir them into the mincemeat and set aside until the pastry
has been made.

Pastry

3 cups of 85% flour
1/3rd to a 1/2 cup of corn oil
cold water to mix
1 pinch of sea salt

Mix all the ingredients together. The less water used and the colder the
water the better the pastry. Make the pastry ahead of time so that it can
sit in the fridge for an hour before being used. Roll the pastry out
between two pieces of greaseproof paper to make it possible to make a
thinner pastry. A little ginger juice can be added to the pastry, this
helps break up the mucous forming nature of baked flour and oil .

Cut and fill the pastry cases with the mincemeat and bake for 30 minutes
at regulo 4.

CHRISTMAS CAKE

3 cups of left over grain
2 cups of cooked bulghar wheat
6 tbsp. of soya flour
2 tbs. w/w flour
2 tbsp. of rice flour
2-3 cups of dried fruit- currants, sultanas or raisins.
2 cups of chopped nuts (Almonds, walnuts)
1 tsp. of ginger juice
1 pinch og cinnamon
2 cups of barley malt
1 tbsp. of barley cup
2 tsp. of umeboshi paste
1 large can of guinness
the rind and juice of one orange and one lemon
1 pinch of sea salt.

Sour the leftover grain by covering it with water and leaving it in a warm
place for 2-3 days. I generally prefer to use rice but b ley or oats are
fine. Soak the dried fruit overnight in the guinness and mix it with the
soured rice the next morning. Cook the bulghar wheat (Approximately 1 cup
of bulghur to 2 cups of water and a pinch of salt). Mix in all the other
ingredients and leave them to rise for several hours or overnight before
cooking. Both soya flour and guinness act as raising agents, and if the
cake is allowed to stand for a while a lighter cake results.

Bake the cake at regulo 2 for 2 1/2- 3 1/2 hours. For a shiny top brush
with a mixture of malt and hot water and cook for a few minutes more. This
cake keeps for about 3 weeks. I find the flavour improves if it is placed
in an air tight container and allowed to sweat for a while.

MARZIPAN SWEETS

Marzipan

2 cups of ground almonds
2-3 tbsp. of barley malt
1 tsp. of lemon juice

Dry roast the almonds until they release a nutty fragrnce. Allow them to cool and mix them with barley malt, lemon juice and a pinch of salt. Knead the marzipan to a uniform consistency and roll it out. Cut into desired shapes- stars, moons, flowers and decorate with small pieces of peel or ginger candy.

Peel

1 orange skin
1 lemon skin
concentrated apple juice
1 pinch of sea salt

Scrub the skins of the orange and lemon and stand them in a bowl with apple juice to cover- in the fridge for about 5 dys. Place the skins in a saucepan of water with enough water to cover, and a pinch of salt and simmer until all the water has been absorbed. Keep the peel in the fridge until you are ready to use it. It will keep for over a month.

PETIT FOURS.

1/4 lb lexia raisins
water to cover
1 pinch of sea salt

pastry

1/2 cup of w/w flour
1/2 cup of rice flour
1 cup of fine or medium oatflakes
6 tbsp. of oil
cold water to mix
1 pinch of sea salt

Simmer the raisins with a pinch of salt for 20-30 minutes, until the water has been absorbed. Puree the raisins in a suribachi and set them aside.

Mix all the pastry ingredients together and allow them to sit in the fridge for an hour. Roll the pastry beween two pieces of greaseproof paper for a thinner pastry and layer half of pastry on the bottom of an oiled baking tray. Spread the raisin puree over the pastry and layer the other half of the pastry on top of this. Bake in a medium oven for 30 minutes or until done. When cool cut into small squares.

Variations. Apricots can be used to make the puree, also fresh apples cooked with a little kuzu. Mincemeat would be delicious too. After cooking the petit fours can be glazed with a thin barley malt kuzu or rice syrup glaze. For variety mix roasted sunflower seeds, almonds or sesame seeds into the glaze before spreading it on the petit fours.

HALVAH

3 cups of sesame seeds
1/2 a cup of barley malt or rice syrup
1 cup of ground almonds
1 pinch of sea salt

Clean, wash and dry roast the sesame seeds until they powder easily when rubbed between the first and the third finger. Grind the seeds very finely in the suribachi. Roast the almonds until they release a nutty fragrance, remove them from the heat and mixing all the ingredients together cook them for several minutes, stirring constantly to prevent sticking. When the ingredients have cooled roll them into little balls and serve with a garnish of a roasted hazelnut.

CHRISTMAS PUDDING

1 loaf of stale yeasted bread
1 bottle of guinness
3 cups of dried fruit
1lb of nuts (walnuts, almonds)
2 cups of soya flour
1 grated carrot
rind of 1 orange
rind of 1 lemon
1 tsp. of ginger juice
1 tsp. of cinnamon
1-2 tbsp. of corn oil
1/4 tsp. of sea salt

Soak the bread in guinness until it is very crumbly. Add all the other ingredients, mixing them very well and leave them to stand overnight. Oil pudding basins and press the mixture in 1" from the top. Cover the surface of the pudding with greaseproof paper. Cover the pudding with a tea towel and tie it very firmly in place with string. Knot the end of the tea towel together on top of the bowl. Place an overturned saucer in the pressure-cooker with 1-2 inches of water and steam for 2-3 hours (6-9 hours if not in a pressure-cooker). Serve with oat cream or apple custard.

DESSERTS FOR CHILDREN

If anything children require dessert slightly more often than adults; the quality of dessert which we offer our children is very important. Often they will be satisfied with a rice cake spread with rice syrup. Children should not be given too much fruit, particularly raw fruit, as this is very weakening to their digestive systems. If giving children fruit it is often best mixed with grain, such as rice pudding or a bulghur wheat or oat dessert; grain for children is ideal cooked very soft and quite watery with hardly any salt at all, especially if your children are under five. This makes the food much less contractive and because children often do not chew their food, soft cooked grain is much more digestible for them. Flour products and baked foods are not very good for children as they are both contractive and weakening to the digestive system. Too many contractive foods stunt a child's physical growth and too many partial grains such as flour prevent a child developing to its optimum mentally and emotionally.

At the same time it is important to use your own judgement of your child's condition and be aware of our daily and seaonal climatic environment. In hot weather or for a yang child fresh fruit kanten can be ideal, or occasionally a few pieces of raw seasonally ripe fruit.

POPCORN BALLS

Using an oil brush coat a heavy lidded saucepan with either sesame or corn oil. Heat the oil on a medium flame so that it gets very hot but doesn't start to smoke. Over-heated in this way oil changes its chemical nature and is no longer a good food for us. When the oil is ready add the pop corn to just cover the surface at the bottom of the pot. The corn when popped always seems to make more than expected so don't go wild. Place the lid on the popcorn quickly and listen. Within about a minute (if the oil has been heated sufficiently) the corn will begin to pop. Shake the pot gently from time to time. This prevents the popcorn from sticking and burning. When the popping has stopped pour the popcorn into a bowl dicarding any that haven't popped properly.

Heat barley malt or rice syrup until it simmers and pour this over the popcorn. Make the popcorn into balls with wet hands. Crisp the sweetener to a toffee by putting it in a medium oven for a few minutes. Don't leave the popcorn in too long otherwise the sweetener can burn and has an unpleasant taste.
    Variations:- you can mix nuts, seeds or raisins with the popcorn before adding the sweetener.

RICE CAKE SMILES

A quick and simple snack or dessert for children. Take a whole, unsalted rice cake for each child. Roast whole almonds and stick them on the cake with a little barley malt, slicing and halving them where necessary. The

children themselves may have pretty good ideas of the type of faces they
would like to make- currants can be used for eyes e.t.c.

Heat barley malt until it simmers and pour over the rice cake faces which
have been put on a lightly oiled baking tray. Put in a medium oven for 2-3
minutes so the sweetener becomes toffee-like when it cools.

    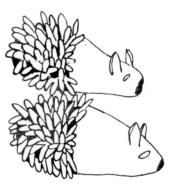

DRIED FRUIT SHAKE

1/2 a cup of dried fruit (apricots, peaches, apples)
2 cups of oat milk
1 or 2 tsp. of rice syrup to taste.

Bring the dried fruit to a boil with enough water to cover it easily.
Simmer with a small pinch of salt until it is soft. If there is any water
left drain this and save it for use in another dish. Mix the fruit and oat
milk and blend in a blender or using a hand whisk. This makes about 3
cups.

COFFEE HEDGEHOGS

3 large ripe pears

3 tsps. of grain coffee (barley cup)
7-8 tbsp. of barley malt.
1/4 lb roasted almonds

Wash and bake the pears in a medium oven for 20-30 minutes. Take the pears
out, allow them to cool and cut the pears in half. Heat the barley malt
and mix in the barley cup. Dip the pears into the barley malt at their
thickest end to half their length, and at their thinnest end just to make
a nose. Place in a medium oven for 2-3 minutes to crisp. Cut the almonds
into long slithers and stick them half in to the malt covered part of the

45

pear. The almonds look like the quills of the hedgehogs. Two more almonds can be cut to the appropriate shape and used for eyes, two more can be ued for the ears.

WALNUT PINWHEELS

2 cups of medium oatflakes
1/2 cup of rice flour
1/2 cup w/w flour
1 small pinch of salt
3 tbsp. of corn oil
cold water to mix

1/4 lb of roasted walnuts
4 tbsp. of barleymalt or rice syrup

Mix the dry pastry ingredients with the oil by hand; add water to mix to a dough consistency and set the pastry aside in the fridge for an hour. Roll the pastry out between greaseproof paper for a thinner pstry.

Roast the walnuts and chop or grind them very fine. Mix in the barleymalt. Roll the pastry to a long rectangle. Spread the walnut and barley malt mixture on the pastry and roll the pastry into a spiral. Make sure the ends are sealed and bake in a medium oven for about 30 minutes. Allow the roll to cool and cut it into spiral rounds.

Centres in England

Deanne Bennett   28 Mentor Street, Longsight, Manchester
Natural Health Centre, Jenny John   27 Regent Street, Brighton
Rod Onisson   9a Madret Street, Faversham, Kent
Daphne Watson   40 The Ridgeway, Marlow Bucks
Keith Phillips   12 Harowdene Road, Bristol
Mike Abrahams   24 Downfield Rcad, Clifton, Bristol
Linda Burns   6 Vineyard, Dartington, Totnes, Devon
Oliver Cowmeadow   The Coach House, Buckyette Farm, Littlehempston, Totnes, Devon
Michele Cowmeadow   14, Cornwall Terrace, Penzance, Cornwall
Steve Thorpe   56, Beech Avenue, Sherwood Rise, Nottingham
Woodbridge Nat. Health Centre   Ivydene, Cliff Road, Waldringfield, Suffolk   Wald. 712
London East West Centre   188 Old Street, London E.C.1. (071) 251 4076

Centres In Scotland

East West Centre   112 St Stephens Stroot, Edinburgh
Chris Stewart   57 Summerhill Crescent, Aberdeen

Books mentioned are available at Genesis Books, Old Street, London (071) 250 1868;
Infinity Books, 25, North Road, Brighton; The Granary, Truro; East West Centre, Edinburgh
and from Cornish Connection at the address below.

Other books published by Cornish Connection

Introduction to Macrobiotics, Oliver Cowmeadow 32 pages £1.50
Macrobiotic Cooking, Michele Cowmeadow 64 pages £3.50
Yin & Yang, Oliver Cowmeadow 84 pages £3.95
Cornish Connection, The Coach House, Buckyette Farm, Littlehempston,
Totnes, Devon TQ9 6ND   Telephone 080426 593